D1246970

In The Beginning

A CHILD IS BORN OUT OF THE
LOVE A MAN AND WOMAN HAVE
FOR ONE ANOTHER, THEIR
DESIRE TO CREATE ANOTHER HUMAN
BEING IN THE IMAGE OF THEIR LOVE.

In The Beginning
בְּרֵאשִׁית

THE JEWISH BABY BOOK

by

Naomi Patz   Jane Perman

Illustrated by Dianne Appleman

National Federation of Temple Sisterhoods
Union of American Hebrew Congregations
New York

IN LOVE, WE DEDICATE
THIS BOOK TO OUR CHILDREN
DEBBY AND AVIVA
DEBBIE AND DANNY
MARC

ISBN 08074-0258-3

Manufactured in the United States of America
10 9 8 7 6 5 4

_____
Name

child of

_____ and _____
Mother   Father

was born on

_____
Day of week

_____
Date   Month   Year

at

_____ o'clock _____ M

Place of birth _____

Registered at _____ Certificate number _____

בָּרוּךְ אַתָּה, יְיָ אֱלֹהֵינוּ, מֶלֶךְ הָעוֹלָם,
שֶׁהֶחֱיָנוּ וְקִיְּמָנוּ וְהִגִּיעָנוּ לַזְּמַן הַזֶּה.

Blessed is our God, Ruler of the universe, for giving us life,
for sustaining us, and for enabling us to reach this day of joy.

God of all generations, You have blessed
our lives with companionship and mutual
love. We are thankful for all Your past
gifts. Now our hearts are full, in this
time of expectant hope.

EXPECTING THE BABY

special preparations, baby showers, thoughts, and anticipations

With the birth of our little one,
help us to be worthy parents, and
bless us with long life together
in family love. Amen.

A NEW LIFE BEGINS

Baby was delivered by _____

Birth weight _____ Length _____ Complexion _____

Color of eyes _____ Color and quantity of hair _____

Comments

זֶה הַיּוֹם עָשָׂה יְיָ; נָגִילָה וְנִשְׂמְחָה בוֹ.

This is the day God has made; let us
rejoice and be glad in it.

EARLIEST IMPRESSIONS

highlights of the delivery, the hospital stay

THE BIRTH IS ANNOUNCED

Source of all life, our hearts are filled
with joy for the new life which has been
entrusted to us. Not with words alone shall
we voice our thanks, but with our striving
to rear our child with love and understanding
and with tender care.

WELCOME HOME

בָּרוּךְ הַבָּא בְּשֵׁם יְיָ.

Blessed are you who come in the name of the Eternal.

Psalms 118:26

THE FAMILY MEETS THE BABY

include the names and ages of brothers and sisters and their response to their first look at the baby; also note the reactions of grandparents, aunts, and uncles to the new arrival

We are thankful for the many joys with which our life has been blessed. Now this great goodness has come to us: a new life, a new child to love, the opening of a new chapter in the chronicle of our family's existence. Oh, may this child grow up in health and happiness to become a blessing to family, friends, and neighbors.

FIRST DAYS

sleep habits, feeding experiences,
bathtime, memorable moments

O small face,
Your bright eyes shine at us
with trust and love.
Your tiny, grasping hands
with perfect nails
curl around our fingers.
What a wondrous work you are!
What responsibility is ours!
May God grant us the wisdom, strength, and courage
to help you become the best that is in you to be.

VISITORS AND GIFTS

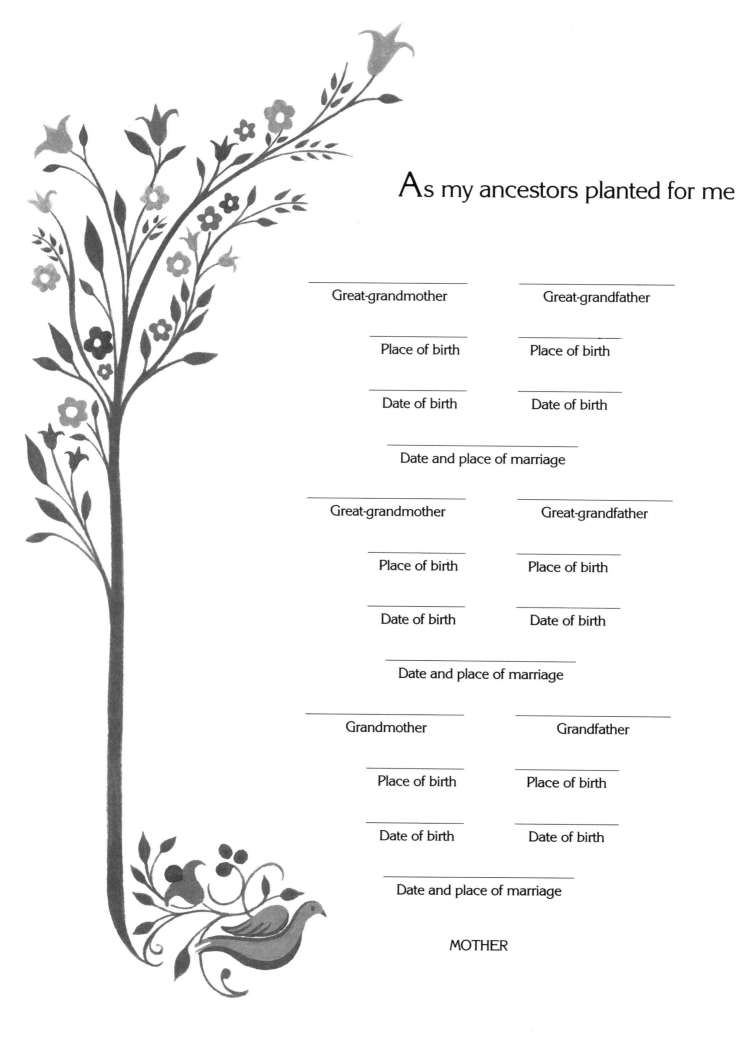

As my ancestors planted for me

_____   _____
Great-grandmother   Great-grandfather

_____   _____
Place of birth   Place of birth

_____   _____
Date of birth   Date of birth

_____
Date and place of marriage

_____   _____
Great-grandmother   Great-grandfather

_____   _____
Place of birth   Place of birth

_____   _____
Date of birth   Date of birth

_____
Date and place of marriage

_____   _____
Grandmother   Grandfather

_____   _____
Place of birth   Place of birth

_____   _____
Date of birth   Date of birth

_____
Date and place of marriage

MOTHER

so do I plant for my children.
Taanit 23a

_____   _____
Great-grandmother   Great-grandfather

_____   _____
Place of birth   Place of birth

_____   _____
Date of birth   Date of birth

_____
Date and place of marriage

_____   _____
Great-grandmother   Great-grandfather

_____   _____
Place of birth   Place of birth

_____   _____
Date of birth   Date of birth

_____
Date and place of marriage

_____   _____
Grandmother   Grandfather

_____   _____
Place of birth   Place of birth

_____   _____
Date of birth   Date of birth

_____
Date and place of marriage

FATHER

_____   _____

Mother   Father

_____   _____   _____   _____

Date of birth   Place of birth   Date of birth   Place of birth

_____

Date and place of marriage

Siblings

_____

Baby's name

In ancient times,
parents planted trees
when children were born:
a pine or cypress for a
daughter, a cedar for a son. When
the children grew up and married,
the poles for their *chupah* (marriage
canopy) were made from the wood
of these same trees. We can mark
this custom today by planting a tree
in Israel in the baby's name through
the Jewish National Fund.

JEWISH LIFE-CYCLE CEREMONIES

Berit Milah

Jews have always celebrated the birth of a child. Since the time of Abraham, circumcision of male infants has been a sign of the covenant between God and the Jewish people. The ceremony of *Berit Milah*—the Covenant of Circumcision—normally takes place on the eighth day after the birth. An important part of the ritual is the official giving of a Hebrew name to the infant. Girls were traditionally named in the synagogue.

Berit Hachayim

Today, in the belief that girls should participate fully in Jewish life and accept the obligations of Judaism, many parents choose to enter their daughters into the covenant in a home ceremony that parallels *Berit Milah* in religious significance. This ceremony is called *Berit Hachayim*—the Covenant of Life—or *Hachnassah Laberit*—Entry into the Covenant.

Naming the Baby

Giving a Hebrew name to a Jewish child is an ancient custom. Many families have a naming ceremony for their son or daughter in the synagogue as a public confirmation of their private observance at home. European Jews (Ashkenazim) and their descendants usually memorialize a deceased relative by selecting a name which honors the memory of that relative (either the exact name or one whose meaning is equivalent to the original). Sephardic Jews, on the other hand, consider it a great honor to give the child the name of a living relative.

(These three ceremonies can be found in the CCAR home prayer book, *Gates of the House.*)

MAY THIS NAME BE BLESSED

_____ , child of _____
Baby's Hebrew name   Mother's and father's Hebrew names

was named at _____
                                    Name and location of synagogue

by _____ on _____
              Name of officiating rabbi   Hebrew and English dates

Baby was named for _____ The baby's name means _____

ENTRY INTO THE COVENANT

the *Berit Milah*
of

_____   _____
Hebrew name   English name

son of

_____ and _____
Father's Hebrew name   Mother's Hebrew name

was held on

_____   _____
Hebrew date   English date

at

_____
Location

…You shall keep My covenant, you and your offspring to come, through the ages. Such shall be My covenant, which you shall keep, between Me and you and your offspring to follow: every male among you shall be circumcised. You shall circumcise the flesh of your foreskin, and that shall be the sign of the covenant between Me and you. At the age of eight days, every male among you throughout the generations shall be circumcised.…

Genesis 17: 9-12

כְּשֵׁם שֶׁנִּכְנַס לַבְּרִית . . .
כֵּן יִכָּנֵס לְתוֹרָה, לְחֻפָּה, וּלְמַעֲשִׂים טוֹבִים.

Even as he entered into the covenant…
So may he enter into the study of Torah, the blessing of marriage, and
the practice of good deeds.

*May the One who blessed our fathers, Abraham, Isaac, and
Jacob, bless this child and keep him from all harm. May we
rear him to dedicate his life in faithfulness to God, his heart
receptive always to Torah and Mitzvot. Then shall he bring
blessing to us, to his people, and to all the world. Amen.*

Circumcision performed by _____

Sandak _____

Godparents _____

Guests

Reflections

כְּשֵׁם שֶׁנִּכְנְסָה לַבְּרִית . . .
כֵּן תִּכָּנֵס לְתוֹרָה, לְחֻפָּה, וּלְמַעֲשִׂים טוֹבִים.

As she has entered into the covenant of life…
So may she enter into the study of Torah,
the blessing of marriage, and the practice of good deeds.

THE COVENANT OF LIFE

Berit Hachayim

Our God, God of all generations, sustain our daughter

_____   _____
        Hebrew name   English name

child of

_____ and _____
      Mother's Hebrew name   Father's Hebrew name

who has entered into the covenant of life

on

_____   _____
        Hebrew date   English date

Names of witnesses

Guests

Reflections

May the One who blessed our mothers,
Sarah, Rebekah, Leah, and Rachel,
bless this child and keep her from
all harm. O God, we give thanks to
You for the gift of our child, who
has entered into the covenant of life.
Teach us to rear her with care and
affection, with wisdom and understanding,
that she may be a faithful child of our
people and a blessing to the world. We
give thanks to You, Eternal One, Source of life. Amen.

SANCTIFICATION OF THE FIRSTBORN CHILD

The birth of a first child evokes a sense of wonder and gratitude. This new life connects parents to the chain of Jewish generations. Many families wish to celebrate the arrival of their firstborn daughter or son with a special ceremony.

An ancient ritual, the *Pidyon Haben*—Redemption of the Son—takes place when a firstborn boy becomes one month old. The Torah commands that the firstborn male of every Jewish mother be consecrated to the service of God. The baby could be redeemed from the obligation of Temple service by the payment of five shekels to a *kohen*, a Temple priest. When Reform Jews stopped praying for the rebuilding of the Temple in Jerusalem and abolished class distinction in Judaism, this symbolic "redemption" ceremony became superfluous.

The impulse to affirm the sanctity of life remains, however, and has been translated into the beautiful ceremony of the Sanctification of the Firstborn. A festive gathering is held on the occasion of the one-month birthday of the firstborn. In the presence of family and friends, the new parents give thanks to God, make a contribution of *tsedakah*, and formally acknowledge their acceptance of the responsibilities of parenthood.

_____   _____
           Hebrew date   English date

A gift of *chai* ($18.00) was contributed to _____ in honor of the sanctification of our firstborn child.

May God bless you and keep you;
May God look kindly upon you and be gracious to you;
May God bestow favor upon you and give you peace. Amen.

                                                Numbers 6: 24-26

Guests

Reflections

FIRST MONTH

There is no joy like the joy of the heart.
Ben Sirach 30:16

Humans stamp many coins from the same mold, and every coin is exactly the same. But God has stamped many people from the same mold, yet no person is like any other. Therefore each person must say "for my sake was the world created."

Sanhedrin 37a

FOR THE RECORD

Physician's name _____

The doctor says

Blood type

Allergies

Childhood illnesses

Other medical events

לְחַיִּים וּלְשָׁלוֹם!

To good health—and a life of peace!

GROWING

Date	Age	Height	Weight	Comments

IMMUNIZATIONS	DATES GIVEN			BOOSTERS		
Diphtheria, Pertussis, Tetanus (DPT)						
Diphtheria, Tetanus, (DT)						
Polio						
Measles						
Rubella						
Mumps						
Tuberculin Test (TBC)						
Others						

רוֹפֵא כָל־בָּשָׂר וּמַפְלִיא לַעֲשׂוֹת.

Wondrous Fashioner and Sustainer of life, Source of our health and our strength, we give You thanks and praise.

BABY TEETH

as each new tooth appears, enter the date and child's age (in months)

Teething

First visit to the dentist

MENUS AND MEALTIME

date begun and baby's reaction

BREAST FEEDING

BOTTLE FEEDING

INTRODUCTION OF SOLIDS

first food

NEW FOODS

We praise You, O Eternal our God, who bring forth bread from the earth.

Berachot 6:1

HOLDS OWN BOTTLE

EATS FROM SPOON

DRINKS FROM CUP

MANAGES FINGER FOODS

HOLDS OWN CUP AND DRINKS

FEEDS SELF WITH SPOON

TOTAL INDEPENDENCE

בָּרוּךְ אַתָּה, יְיָ אֱלֹהֵינוּ, מֶלֶךְ הָעוֹלָם, הַמּוֹצִיא לֶחֶם מִן הָאָרֶץ.

EARLIEST TRIUMPHS

describe, including date and baby's age

RESPONDS

    to voice

    to light

VISUALLY FOLLOWS A MOVING OBJECT

TURNS HEAD WHILE ON STOMACH

LIFTS HEAD

SMILES

LAUGHS

REACHES FOR AN OBJECT

TURNS OVER

    from stomach to back

    from back to stomach

FIRST SLEEPS THROUGH THE NIGHT

We thank You, God, for granting us the joy of seeing this infant, our child, develop. May these first exciting moments of growth be the beginnings of a lifetime of accomplishment in Your service and for the sake of humanity. Amen.

SITS

with support

alone

RAISES SELF FROM LYING TO SITTING POSITION

CRAWLS

STANDS

with support

pulls self up

alone

WALKS

with support

first steps

alone

EXPLORING

in the house

outdoors

EXCURSIONS

in the neighborhood

other trips

FAVORITE PLAYTHINGS, SONGS, AND NURSERY RHYMES

RELATES TO PARENTS, SIBLINGS, RELATIVES, AND FRIENDS

REACTS TO "STRANGERS"

Reflections

If one learns as a child, what is one like?
Like ink written on clean paper.

Pirke Avot 4:25

FROM THE MOUTHS OF BABES...

Psalms 8:3

Children become especially dear to their parents when they begin to talk.

Tanchuma Tetsaveh

include date, child's age, and details

First sounds

First words

Identifies objects in pictures

First says own name

Early sentences

"Helps" recite nursery rhyme

Memorable pronunciations

Recites alphabet

Counts to ten

First Hebrew word

WORTH QUOTING

ideas, questions, and clever expressions
date and child's age

One who is descended from you often teaches you.
Yevamot 63a

GROWING OLDER

physical skills, artistic and imaginative play
date and child's age

ACTIVITIES

indoors

outdoors

narrow escapes

FAVORITE TOYS, PLAYTHINGS, AND GAMES

Hear, my child, the instruction of your father,
And forsake not the teaching of your mother.
Proverbs 1:8

*A garden of God
is our childhood,
each day a festival
radiant with laughter and play.*
M. J. Lebensohn, *Hayaldut*

FAVORITE SONGS, BOOKS, RECORDS, AND TELEVISION PROGRAMS

PLAYMATES

ANIMAL FRIENDS

Teach children the way they should go,
And even when they are old,
They will not depart from it.

Proverbs 22:6

STEPS TO INDEPENDENCE ("I can do it myself!")

NAPS AND BEDTIME

from crib to bed

TOILET TRAINING

RELATES TO FAMILY AND FRIENDS

EXCURSIONS

in the neighborhood

longer trips

REJOICE IN YOUR FESTIVALS

Deuteronomy 16:14

Celebrating holidays and life-cycle events together makes the year special. Shared ceremonies and experiences enrich family life and build a sense of belonging to the Jewish people.

Chanukah   חֲנֻכָּה

helps light candles...sings the blessings...sings holiday songs ...opens presents...spins the *sevivon* (*dreidel*)...eats *latkes*

Tu Bishvat טִ״יּו בִּשְׁבָט

plants a tree in Israel…plants seeds and watches them grow…eats fruits that grow in Israel

Purim פּוּרִים

wears a costume…twirls the *grogger*…eats *hamantashen*…hears the *megillah* read in synagogue…goes to a Purim carnival

Pesach   פֶּסַח

eats *matzah*…sits at the *seder*…sings *"Dayenu"*…finds the *afikoman*…
asks the Four Questions

Yom Ha'atsmaut   יוֹם הָעַצְמָאוּת
(Israel Independence Day)

watches a parade...identifies the Israeli flag

Lag Ba'omer   לַ״ג בָּעֹמֶר

goes on a picnic...takes a nature walk

Shavuot   שָׁבוּעוֹת

arranges flowers for the holiday table...helps say the blessings for new fruits
of the season

BIRTHDAY CELEBRATIONS

anecdotes, photographs, favorite presents, and friends

Youth is a garland of flowers
Shabbat 152a

FAMILY CELEBRATIONS

describe special occasions, including dates and photographs

When you teach your children and grandchildren Torah, it is as if you have yourself been given the Torah at Mt. Sinai. And God told all of Israel: Set these words, which I command you this day, upon your heart….Teach them faithfully to your children.

שְׁמַע יִשְׂרָאֵל: יְיָ אֱלֹהֵינוּ, יְיָ אֶחָד!

Hear, O Israel: the Eternal is our God,
the Eternal is One!

Deuteronomy 6:4

FIRST PRAYER

VISITING THE SYNAGOGUE

include dates, occasions, name of synagogue, the names of the rabbi and cantor, child's reactions and remarks

This we will do...

as our mothers and fathers have done in every age, as our own parents did with us, we bring our child to Your House to study Your Law, to be among those who seek to know Your ways and to follow the path of Your *Mitzvot.* We pray that this child will grow in heart and mind, and—through wisdom and knowledge—perform deeds of mercy and justice, ennobling the life of all Your children.

ON
ENTERING
RELIGIOUS SCHOOL

Date

Name and location of synagogue

Teacher's name

Child's reaction

Date of consecration

Comments

Your children are the best surety;
better than prophets and patriarchs; for their sake I give you the Torah.

Shir Hashirim Rabbah I, 4

FIRST
DAY OF SCHOOL

Date

Name and location of school

Teacher's name

Child's reaction

Classmates

Comments

So fast,
So soon,
With eager steps
They run to greet their future.
Does she hesitate?
Will he look back?
Who would have imagined...
Where has the time gone?

Days should speak and passing years should teach wisdom.

Job 32:7

REFLECTIONS

בָּרוּךְ אַתָּה, יְיָ אֱלֹהֵינוּ, מֶלֶךְ הָעוֹלָם,
שֶׁהֶחֱיָנוּ וְקִיְּמָנוּ וְהִגִּיעָנוּ לַזְּמַן הַזֶּה.

Blessed is our God, Ruler of the universe, for giving us life,
for sustaining us, and for enabling us to reach this day of joy.